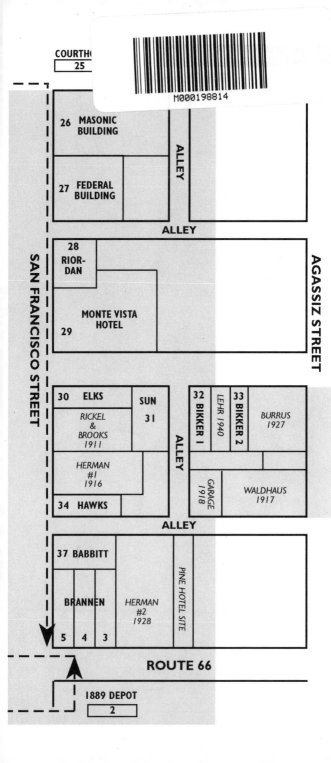

COURTHO[USE]
25

M000198814

26 MASONIC BUILDING

27 FEDERAL BUILDING

ALLEY

ALLEY

28 RIOR-DAN

MONTE VISTA HOTEL
29

SAN FRANCISCO STREET

AGASSIZ STREET

30 ELKS

RICKEL & BROOKS 1911

SUN
31

HERMAN #1 1916

34 HAWKS

32 BIKKER I

LEHR 1940

33 BIKKER 2

BURRUS 1927

ALLEY

GARAGE 1918

WALDHAUS 1917

ALLEY

37 BABBITT

BRANNEN

HERMAN #2 1928

PINE HOTEL SITE

5 4 3

ROUTE 66

1889 DEPOT
2

Printed by Northland Printing
Flagstaff, Arizona
On Recycled Paper

Cover: Design by Joan Carstensen
Northland Printing,
Photograph by
Sherry Mangum

Table of Contents

Map

Buildings Discussed
[Those With Photos in Brackets]

Introduction

In this beautifully done volume, Dick and Sherry Mangum have scored again in their series of handbooks for hikers and bikers.

Their first book, *Flagstaff Hikes*, appeared in April, 1992, and was so enthusiastically received that it went into a revised, enlarged edition within two months, retitled *Flagstaff Hikes and Mountain Bike Rides*. A few months later they published *Sedona Hikes and Mountain Bike Rides*, filling another need.

This new book, *Flagstaff Historic Walk*, takes the walker-reader through the downtown area guided by carefully drafted maps and drawings plus old photos of the structures, faced by current ones. With each building there appear dates and other interesting data on construction and remodelings, original and present uses, and architectural style.

With this guide, downtown comes clearly into focus for newcomers as well as older residents. It offers in pleasing, interesting form a significant slice of community history, and for those seeking further details, there is a brief but adequate bibliography.

Dick and Sherry have not only produced a fun-guide book for the growing numbers of walkers, but have performed a major service to the cause of historic preservation and restoration by generating, with this pleasing approach a better understanding of what is referred to in very general terms as "old downtown."

Platt Cline

Flagstaff, Arizona, March, 1993

(NOTE: Platt Cline was for thirty years the editor of the *Arizona Daily Sun*, Flagstaff's newspaper. Since his retirement nineteen years ago, he has devoted himself to writing about Flagstaff history, producing the definitive works, *They Came to the Mountain, Mountain Campus,* and *The View From Mountain Campus.* His new book, *Mountain Town*, carrying the history of Flagstaff to the present, will be released in 1993.)

Foreword

We love Flagstaff and think that its historic downtown district is a fascinating place.

Because of the way Flagstaff developed, many of its historic buildings were solidly constructed of masonry: stone, concrete and brick. The buildings have been modernized with coats of stucco or other coverings, but they have managed to keep most of their integrity.

In 1979 the Railroad Addition Historic District was designated and its boundaries were marked so that buildings within the district could qualify for inclusion in the National Register of Historic Places. (The shaded portion of the map shows the district). We felt that it was logical to have our walking tour within the boundaries of this district and it worked out very well, resulting in a nice walk with plenty to see.

The buildings within the district have stories, and we realized as we researched this book that the buildings and the people connected with them tell the history of Flagstaff in an appealing and interesting way.

Recently it seemed that downtown Flagstaff might die as have so many downtowns. Shopping centers and chain stores took so much business away that vacancies dotted the area.

Today there is renewed interest in downtown Flagstaff. Great improvements have already been made in the district—Jim Babbitt's restoration of the Babbitt Brothers Building is a magnificent example—and other plans are on the drawing board. We believe that downtown Flagstaff will become more and more interesting, an even better place for you to stroll around in and visit.

We hope that this book will turn you into a lover of downtown Flagstaff too.

About the Authors

Richard K. Mangum was born in Flagstaff in 1936. After attending local schools, he received a law degree from the University of Arizona and returned to Flagstaff to practice law. Following fifteen years as a lawyer, he became a judge of the superior court of Coconino County in 1976.

From his childhood Dick has been fascinated by the history of Flagstaff, reading with enthusiasm all the historical materials he could locate and drawing upon the recollections of his late father, H. Karl Mangum, who moved to Flagstaff in 1931.

He is a member of Flagstaff's Historic Sites Commission.

Sherry G. Mangum came to Flagstaff when she was seven years old and has been interested in Flagstaff history since she was a child. Her mother and father are professional photographers who took her on many trips around the area, and she developed an appreciation of the Flagstaff landscape and its history.

Rather than trying to produce an exact duplicate of the old scenes in her photographs for this book, Sherry has depicted them as the modern visitor sees them.

Dick and Sherry have previously written *Flagstaff Hikes and Mountain Bike Rides,* and *Sedona Hikes and Mountain Bike Rides,* best-selling local books.

Acknowledgments

We wish to thank the following people for their help on this book:

Jeffe Aronson for inspiration*; Donna Ashworth, Jim Babbitt, Platt Cline* and *Henry Giclas* for proofreading and consultation.

We give a special thanks to *Platt Cline* for writing the Introduction.

Photo Credits

Arizona Historical Society Northern Division:
> Pages: 14, 18, 20, 32, Back Flap, Front Flap

Jim Babbitt:
> Pages: 12, 40

Cline Library, NAU, Special Collections:
> Pages: 16, 24, 46, 48, 50, 58

Sherry Mangum:
> Front Cover, Pages: 13, 15, 17, 19, 21, 25, 27, 29, 33, 35, 37, 39, 41, 43, 45, 47, 49, 51, 53, 55, 59, Back Flap, Front Flap

Silver Fox Studio:
> Pages: 28, 36, 38, 52, 54

Dick and Miriam Wiser:
> Pages: 26, 34, 42, 44, Front Flap and Back Cover

Flagstaff Time Line

The Historic Building Period Is Shaded

900-1100	Sinagua Indians
1540-1700	Spanish Explorers
1830-1840	A. Leroux, Mountain Men
1847	Mexican War
1848	New Mexico Acquired
1851	Sitgreaves Expedition
1853	Whipple Expedition
	Gadsden Purchase
1854	Aubrey Expedition
1857-9	Beale Expedition, Beale Road
1864	Arizona Created
1867	Palmer Surveys Railroad
1876	Boston Party Makes Staff
1876	First White Settlers
1880	Work on Railroad Begins
1881	Old Town, Flagstaff Named
1882	Railroad Arrives
1883	Move to New Town
1886-87-88	Fires Destroy New Town
	Downtown Rebuilt
1891	Coconino County Created
	Flagstaff is County Seat
1894	Flagstaff Becomes a Town
	County Courthouse Built
	Lowell Observatory Opens
1899	Normal School Opens (NAU)
1912	Arizona Becomes a State
1917-18	U.S. in World War I.
1920-24	Postwar Depression
1925	Economic Recovery Starts
1926	Flagstaff Becomes a City
1926-29	Roaring Twenties
1930-40	Great Depression
1941-1945	U.S. in World War II
1946-1970	Flagstaff Is a Regional Hub
1970-1988	Downtown Withers
1988-	Downtown Renaissance

How Flagstaff Got Its Name

In 1876, the Boston Party, a group of men who had been lured West by irresponsible promises of finding a land of milk and honey in northern Arizona, gave up an attempt to settle along the Little Colorado near present-day Winslow. They decided to try their luck in Prescott and on their way, they made camp at Antelope Spring in a mountain valley on the Fourth of July.

Properly patriotic, they stripped a pine tree of branches and bark and hung Old Glory at its top. The stripped tree was used as a marker for the spring by travelers afterwards, who referred to the place as the spring by the flag staff. A few sheep ranchers settled in the region, and gradually the area became known as Flag Staff, then Flagstaff.

As advance crews of the Atlantic & Pacific Railroad reached Flag Staff in 1880, a tent camp developed near Old Town Spring to supply the railroad workers. When the camp became a hamlet large enough to qualify for a post office, it was necessary for it to have an official name. The citizens of the community held a meeting in 1881 and named the village Flagstaff.

Flagstaff's Moveable Post Office

Flagstaff's Post Office moved five times within the downtown district. Keep your eye on the Post Office symbol as you make this tour and you will find the five locations.

Flagstaff Block Plan

300 feet

The original townsite of Flagstaff was laid out according to this plan. Lots are only 25 feet wide, but they are 150 feet long, with footage trimmed off the back for the alleys. This accounts for the long narrow buildings you will see, especially those along Route 66.

Building Materials

The obvious first material choice was lumber, as Flagstaff sits in the heart of the largest Ponderosa pine forest in the world. Recurring fires, however, led to the passage of a law in 1897 that required masonry construction downtown.

The area's volcanoes (Flagstaff lies in the second largest volcanic field in the U.S.) contributed tufa (tuff), a volcanic ash that is compressed under such heat and pressure that it becomes stone. Tufa is a rough, gray material—not very attractive, but durable.

Under the volcanic ash and lava lie the gift of ancient seas: huge beds of sandstone, including the lovely red Moencopi, that was used extensively throughout the historic district. Tufa and Moencopi were locally quarried.

Finally there was brick. Flagstaff brickworks turned out a smooth red brick.

Map Number 1:
Santa Fe Depot

Constructed: 1925
Style: Revival Tudor
Original Use: Train Depot

We think this building is a great place to start our walking tour for three reasons: (1) it is [or will become] the Visitor's Center where you can get Flagstaff information, (2) it symbolizes the railroad and its importance to the development of Flagstaff, and (3) it is one of the most interesting buildings in town.

In 1924, town leaders, including many of the people we will meet on this tour, convinced Santa Fe officials that the time had come for a new railroad depot. The Santa Fe, which was then a very profitable operation, agreed and set its architects to work. They came up with a plan for a building that was unlike any other in Flagstaff, an imposing Revival Tudor edifice, that would be a showpiece. The construction crews went to work in the spring of 1925 and by the end of the year the beautiful new building was almost ready. The grand opening was held on January 5, 1926. The depot has been a symbol of Flagstaff ever since.

As we leave this interesting place, we embark on a tour that will take you to the important buildings of Flagstaff's formative years and will show you our history.

You will find that Flagstaff was never a one-

Between Leroux & San Francisco Streets South of Route 66

Remodeled: None
Style: Same
Present Use: Amtrak Depot & Visitor Center

industry town like Jerome with its mines. Diversity buffered economic swings and prevented a single interest from gaining control. Lumber, livestock and the railroad were the basic industries, and even within the livestock industry there was a balance between cattle and sheep. Added to these was tourism, which continually grew. Due to its strategic location Flagstaff was and is a shopping and transportation hub.

Flagstaff became a county seat and a regional headquarters for other governmental offices such as the Forest Service. These employers furnished a stable payroll and set high working standards.

The early leaders had the foresight to establish a college here (now Northern Arizona University), giving Flagstaff the amenities of a "college town." It is impossible to overestimate the value of having had educated people in the community at the college and at institutions such as Lowell Observatory.

In addition to this diversity of economic base, Flagstaff attracted high quality settlers. There were no robber barons. The men who made fortunes here stayed and built the town.

Map Number 2:
1889 Santa Fe Depot

Constructed: 1889
Style: Commercial
Original Use: Train Depot

Before the railroad came, Flagstaff, for all its natural beauty and its timber, grass and water, was an empty quarter of the United States. Mountain Men had been through the region in the 1830s and 1840s, (notably Antoine Leroux, for whom Leroux Street is named) and in 1857 the Federal Beale Expedition came through here mapping a roadway across Arizona from New Mexico to California; so the region became known—but not occupied. Even after 1859, when Beale had developed his route into a usable roadway, the area was traveled but not inhabited.

The Civil War interrupted exploration of the area. When it ended, Congress decided to open the West by granting to qualified railroad companies every odd section of land on a forty mile swath bracketing the railroad rights of way. Stimulated by these enormous land grants, investors pushed rails to the Pacific along three main lines: the Northern Pacific, the Central Pacific and the Southern Pacific. The Atlantic and Pacific Railway Company was organized in 1866 to tie into the Southern Pacific, but construction stalled and it was not until 1880 that it pushed west from Albuquerque.

South of Route 66, Just East of San Francisco Street

Remodeled: None
Style: Commercial
Present Use: Storage

The railroad made deals with several subcontractors to grade the roadbed, and gangs of men were soon at work. Close behind them came the tie cutters, the steel layers and others.

Everyone knew the train would come through this area and stop for water at present-day Flagstaff. In anticipation, a tiny tent camp developed near Old Town Spring. Railroad crews neared the area in 1881 and found that the camp was the only place to buy supplies and get a drink for miles, and soon they were pouring payroll money into the place. A delay caused by bridging Canyon Diablo kept the crews in the vicinity a long time, and the camp prospered. The inhabitants, believing that a lasting settlement had taken root and would survive after the crews moved on, picked a name for their place, **Flagstaff.** (See page 10).

The rails reached Flagstaff on August 1, 1882, the first depot was set up in a boxcar, and Flagstaff became an active station on the line, with access to the entire East. The rails were advanced to California in 1883, opening Flagstaff's access to the West, and Flagstaff joined the world.

A depot built in 1886 burned in 1888 and this depot was built to replace it, serving until 1926.

Constructed: 1883-1887
Style: Commercial
Original Use: Stores & Office

Building number 5, the oldest in downtown Flagstaff, and **P. J. Brannen,** the man who built it, tell the tale of Flagstaff's earliest settlement. As the Atlantic and Pacific Railroad approached the Flagstaff area, it created opportunity. Some men took advantage of this opportunity by working on the rail crews; others supplied them. P. J. Brannen and his uncle P. B. Brannen, who were successful merchants in Prescott, gambled that the future Flagstaff, then a tent camp on the line, would become a town. They sold out in Prescott and moved their goods to the tiny new settlement, setting up a general store in 1881.

At that time the few homes and stores here were located in what came to be called Old Town, which is to the west of today's town, at the base of Mars Hill, see p. 63. The Brannens started their store there in a tent. The store succeeded, and in a short time they replaced the tent with a log structure. When the railroad located its depot east of Old Town in 1883, P. J. Brannen decided that the Brannens would move their store half a mile east to a better site on a broad flat area north of the depot. Thus he became the prime mover in creating New Town, the present Flagstaff.

Remodeled: 1917, 1927
Style: Commercial
Present Use: Saloon, Stores

P. J. Brannen's New Town store is Building 5. It was made of stone and although fires continued to burn buildings, the stones survived them all. P. B. Brannen constructed Building 4 next door, and P.B.'s brother D. J. Brannen, Flagstaff's first physician, erected Building 3, where he had a drug store and his medical office. The original stone is now covered by brick or other facing materials.

All the Brannens were active in Flagstaff's early life, but P. J. seemed to contribute the most. In addition to spurring the move to New Town, he sparked the official adoption of "Flagstaff" as the name of the town in 1881, and led the effort to create the first school in 1882. The land where the first Catholic church was built was donated by him and he was one of its leading members. He was instrumental in the formation of Coconino County in 1891. Before Flagstaff was incorporated, P. J. was its informal Mayor and Postmaster.

Brannen prospered until the Panic of 1893, which strapped him and made him unable to compete successfully with the new Babbitt Brothers store. In 1894 he sold out to the Babbitts and left the town he had helped found, moving to California, where he died in 1939.

Constructed: 1888
Style: Victorian Commercial
Original Use: Saloon

In many railroad towns the original center of commerce develops along the railroad tracks, and this was true for Flagstaff. After P. J. Brannen led the move to New Town in 1883 and anchored it with his store, (Building 5) a number of buildings were constructed along Front Street (now Route 66) between San Francisco and Leroux Streets. The heart of early Flagstaff was this block along Route 66 that you are now walking.

While the original business establishments in Old Town were set up in tents, when the citizens moved to New Town, they erected more substantial wooden buildings. Fire was a terrible hazard in those first years. Open flames were everywhere—in wood burning stoves and oil lamps—and there was no water system for fighting fires. The wooden buildings were always at risk.

In 1886, 1887 and 1888, blazes swept through the district, causing ferocious damage. Owners rebuilt with masonry, hoping it would be more fire-resistant. The resulting masonry buildings were strong as well as fire-resistant, and many remain today.

Hidden underneath the 1935 add-on Art Deco exterior on this building is the grand old brick

Address:
1 N. San Francisco Street

Remodeled: 1939
Style: Art Deco
Present Use: Shops

building you see in the historical photo. It was erected by **James Vail**.

Vail came to Flagstaff in 1882 and followed two pursuits successfully: business and ranching. He became a saloon owner on this corner and developed it into one of Flagstaff's most popular spots, known as the Parlor Saloon. In the 1890s he went into ranching with his brother-in-law, George Black. Together Vail and Black bought immense tracts of land and large herds of cattle.

In 1901 the two men dissolved their partnership, with Vail taking over the ranching operation. Black got the saloon and ran it for years under the name Black's Bar, changing it to a pool hall during Prohibition. It stayed in the Black family until 1944.

Vail continued ranching and was active in town affairs as well as business. He was on the Town Council, the Territorial Legislature and the County Board of Supervisors. By 1904 he was one of the largest ranchers in Flagstaff. That year he suffered a broken leg that never healed properly, and Vail was facing its amputation.

Vail went into Babbitt Brothers' store in April 1906, bought a gun and shot himself to death.

Constructed: 1888
Style: Victorian Commercial
Original Use: Saloon

Like the Vail Building, the Donahue Building was built as a saloon.

The railroad construction crews were full of rough young men who poured into Flagstaff to spend their wages in the saloons. The Prescott newspaper reported that conditions were so rowdy that Flagstaff had a place "...*in which the proprietor has a large platform erected which he has furnished with several pistols and guns. When a valiant gets a little troublesome he picks him off at a single shot and that is the end of the creature.*"

Wide-open gambling games ran around the clock, and brawls and shootings were frequent.

The men who ran these saloons had to be brave and strong and ready to handle any kind of trouble. This building was erected by one of the most successful saloon keepers, **Jerome J. "Sandy" Donahue**, who called it the Senate Saloon. Donahue was a large, tough jovial Irishman who lived life to the hilt. Though he could stop a disturbance with a blow of his huge fist, he was warm-hearted and generous and had many friends.

Henry F. Ashurst, a native son of Flagstaff who became a United States Senator, described Donahue as "... *the local celebrity at Flagstaff,*

Address:
22 E. Route 66

Remodeled: 1930s
Style: Commercial
Present Use: Saloon

where he gathered objects d'art, kept a carriage, drank vintages, wore clothing cut a la mode, was sheriff of his county. Of his revenues derived from his Senate Saloon and his gaming tables, he gave bountifully to the needy and helpless."

In addition to running games, Donahue loved to gamble himself. He was once seen to lose $1,000 ($20,000 in 1993 dollars) on the turn of a card and shrug it off with a laugh.

All the other photographs we have chosen for this book show exterior shots of the buildings. Since the photo on page 18 gives a nice view of the outside of the Donahue Building (note the fancy balcony, long since vanished), we thought it would be interesting to show what the inside of one of these saloons looked liked in the rip-roaring days of the past. You can see the drinkers on the left side of the room and the gamblers on the right side.

Donahue is the second man from the front leaning against the bar. The original photo is blurred.

Donahue died broke in 1932, the victim of his overabundant generosity and of Prohibition, which Arizona adopted effective January 1, 1915, before it became a national law.

Map #8. Bender Building
20 E. Route 66
1888

This old building was constructed to house a saloon. The first owner of the property was D. A. Murphy, who had owned a general store in Old Town. A fire wiped out this store; so he moved to New Town and went into the bar business in a wooden building on this site.

Following the fire of 1888, Murphy, along with his neighboring saloon owners, Donahue and Vail, rebuilt with brick.

The appearance of three saloons in a row here gave this corner the unsavory name of Saloon Row, and respectable citizens shunned the area.

In 1924, after Prohibition had closed the bars, Joe Bender bought this property and it became the home of Bender's Cafe. Bender remodeled, tearing out the old front and replacing it with a new face.

Map #9. Brown Building
8 E. Route 66
1899

It is hard to tell the age of this building from its present appearance. It looks as if it is about the same age as its neighbor to the east, but in fact it is much older.

The building was constructed in 1899 and like so many, was used as a saloon. The Babbitts acquired it after Prohibition. For many years afterwards it was the Eagle Grocery Store, operated by Babbitt Lessees. Sullivan's Grocery replaced the Eagle.

In 1924 the Babbitts sold the building to J. C. Brown, who ran a curio shop here, and although Brown came into the picture rather late, the building bears his name in the historic register.

Map #10. Berry Building
1888
See the article on page 24.

Map #11. Aubineau Building
2-4 E. Route 66
1912

This prime corner has been occupied by a store building of some kind throughout New Town's history. Julius Aubineau bought the property in 1898 and leased it to the Flagstaff Commercial Co., a general store. In 1901 he leased it to Pulliam and Vail, clothing merchants.

Julius Aubineau died in 1903 and the place went to his widow, who married Fred Hensing. Mr. Hensing and successors ran a pharmacy here for decades.

Julius Aubineau is known as the Father of Flagstaff's Water System. After the move to New Town in 1883, the citizens continued to use Old Town Spring, but it was not a suitable source of water for more than a small group of people. If the town was to grow, and particularly if there was ever to be a reliable source of water for fire fighting, the community would have to find a large and reliable water supply.

The snow-capped San Francisco Peaks were the obvious answer, but citizens were reluctant to shoulder the cost of building many miles of pipeline to bring water from the mountains to town. When Julius Aubineau was Mayor in 1898, he inspired the townspeople to build the water system, which was successfully done.

There is a monument to him at the Pioneers Historical Museum, see page 62.

The present building was built in 1912, after fire had destroyed four previous ones.

Constructed: 1888
Style: Victorian
Original Use: Saloon

In this building occurred one of the bloodiest episodes in Flagstaff's rowdy days, a real chapter out of the book of the Wild West.

On January 18, 1887 two brothers, George and William Hawks, were carousing and drinking in the San Juan Saloon located here. George got into a fight with a cowboy. William gave George a gun and taunted him to use it, whereupon George pistol-whipped the cowboy and ran. The California Kid grabbed George as he tried to leave the bar. At this point the saloon owner, John Berry, tried to wrestle the gun away from George. It went off, giving Berry a mortal wound.

Berry was a very popular man, a Flagstaff pioneer, and his death hit the community hard. Even though the Hawks boys were sons of J. F. "Dad" Hawks, one of the earliest settlers, who enjoyed an excellent reputation, a mob sentiment against the boys flared up.

The Hawks brothers were arrested and taken around the corner to the jail, then located at 16 N. Leroux. Fearing mob action, the Sheriff put two deputies on guard. The mob appeared a few hours later with a lynch rope, threatening to shoot the deputies if they did not give them access to the

Remodeled: 1934
Style: Commercial
Present Use: Cafe

prisoners. The deputies gave in, whereupon the mob went into the cells and shot the brothers.

Pete Berry, John's brother, was notified of John's death. He left his home in Chicago and jumped on the train, headed toward Flagstaff to avenge his brother. When he arrived he found that the killers had already been shot. He stayed, bought the saloon from John's widow, and replaced John's wooden building with a brick one.

Like many who came to Arizona, Pete Berry wished to make a fortune in mining. He located a copper lode at the Grand Canyon, but like all who tried mining in the area, he found it unprofitable. Mining was never a source of wealth in Flagstaff as it was in so much of the West.

Determined to make something of the property, Berry named the trail to his mine Grandview, advertised it as a tourist attraction and built the Grandview Hotel at the top, thus becoming a founder of the tourism industry in Flagstaff. Until the Santa Fe Railroad built its line to the Grand Canyon in 1901 and opened the El Tovar Hotel in 1905, Berry's hotel was the premier Grand Canyon attraction, the destination of the Flagstaff to Grand Canyon Stagecoach.

Map Number 12:
McMillan Building

Constructed: 1886
Style: Victorian
Original Use: Hotel

As we turn this corner on our walk, we turn away from the lawless and brawling history of the "Front Street" bars and move into the more civilized aspects of Flagstaff's life.

You will see a bronze plaque on the exterior wall of this old building, showing that it was built in 1886, by Thomas F. McMillan.

Thomas McMillan was an adventurous man. Born in Tennessee, he tired of life on a farm and set out to see the world. Gold fever sent him first to California and then to Australia, where he learned the art of raising sheep. Armed with this knowledge he returned to California and became a sheep rancher, building up a large herd. A series of droughts hit California in the 1870s, causing many ranchers to move elsewhere.

Literally looking for greener pastures, McMillan drove his sheep to the area which was to become Flagstaff in 1876, finding virgin grasslands and suitable water. There was open range, so a rancher could locate his stock anywhere he chose and did not have to pay for pasturage. The local grasses were very nutritious, and the sheep thrived. The major problem for the sheepman was not production but getting goods to market. The hub of

the American wool market was Boston, and there were only two ways to reach it from Arizona, since there were no railroads in the territory—go east to the nearest rail point at Trinidad, Colorado; or go west to the Colorado River, then transport goods by boat around Cape Horn. As a result, the sheepmen did not try to sell their meat, only the wool.

The arrival of the railroad in 1882 made it possible for ranchers to ship meat as well as wool and brought all shipping costs down. Flush with new profits from ranching, McMillan decided in 1886 that the town needed a first class fireproof hotel and built this one of masonry. The outside walls are of native stone, with locally made brick inside. The brickyard was located where the present Public Library stands.

As soon as the building was completed, the Arizona Central Bank became a tenant. The names "Bank" and "Hotel" were displayed on the roof under separate peaks, and the operation was known as the Bank Hotel.

In 1892 it became the terminus for the Flagstaff to Grand Canyon Stagecoach, running its passengers to Pete Berry's Grandview Hotel.

Map Number 13:
Dr. Raymond's Office

Constructed: 1911
Style: Renaissance Revival
Original Use: Doctor's Office

The story of this building is the story of **Doctor R.O. Raymond**, who came to Flagstaff in 1908 as the physician for the Arizona Lumber and Timber Company.

In those days educated men were a scarce commodity on the frontier. Doctors could make a comfortable living in cities and there were few who were willing to endure the hardships of the small western towns. Many towns were without physicians. Doctor D. J. Brannen, for example, used to ride the Santa Fe line east and west of Flagstaff on a regular basis, serving the outlying communities. These medical men were of great importance in protecting the health and lives of the pioneers and in bringing culture and civilization to the places where they served.

Raymond was from Illinois and came west for his health, as he suffered from tuberculosis. He found that the Flagstaff climate improved his health. He soon left his position at the lumber mill and opened his own office, which he built on this site.

One of his patients was a sheep rancher who mentioned to the doctor one day that he had more grazing allotment than he could fill, as he had no

Remodeled: None
Style: Same
Present Use: Antique Store

money to buy additional sheep. The doctor invested in sheep with him, liked the business and went into it on his own as a major sheep rancher.

Over the years he amassed very large land holdings, as he was a man who "bought fast and sold slow." Raymond was a shrewd man with money. He invested his medical practice profits not only in real estate but in stocks, mortgages and other investments, gradually building up an estate that was appraised at over $1,500,000 when he died in 1959.

Raymond was well-loved for his kindness, often performing free services for those who could not pay him. He enjoyed exploring the area and would collect seeds of various flowers and grasses, scattering them in likely places to see whether they would grow. Many a colorful nook around Flagstaff owes its wildflowers to his caring hand.

Doctor Raymond never married. He endowed the Raymond Foundation, the chief purpose of which is to support education in Flagstaff. The foundation has contributed thousands of dollars to education and other worthy activities.

This building has the reputation of being haunted.

Map #14. Loy Building
15 N. Leroux Street
1897

This tiny building seems almost too small to have been worth constructing, but here it has been for almost one hundred years.

Loy, the man who constructed the building, was a lawyer, and the place would have been large enough for a one-man law office.

Map #15. Citizen's Bank Building
1903

See the article on page 32.

Map #16. Telephone Exchange
19 N. Leroux Street
1909

This building was constructed by John W. Weatherford, whom you will meet at Building 17.

The first telephone system in Flagstaff was a local system only. The Babbitt Brothers were instrumental in developing it in 1888. By 1909, Flagstaff was ready for statewide telephone service, causing the Overland Telephone Company to come to town. Weatherford built this office as its headquarters.

Not long afterwards, American Telephone & Telegraph took over the company, giving Flagstaff nationwide connections.

The building is constructed of Moencopi sandstone but when the phone company moved out in 1930, the exterior was covered over with stucco. It has been a cafe since.

Map #17. Weatherford Hotel
1898-1899

See article on page 34.

Map #18. Orpheum Theatre
15 W. Aspen Avenue
1916

The ever-enterprising Babbitt Brothers brought the forerunner of movies to Flagstaff at the turn of the century, when they gave magic lantern shows in their Opera House on the top floor of Building 23.

John Weatherford was the father of Flagstaff's first true cinema, however. He built the Majestic Theater here in 1911. True to the conventions of his day, he called it an Opera House.

On New Year's Eve, December 31, 1915, there was a huge snowfall in Flagstaff that caved in the roof of the Majestic.

Weatherford immediately undertook to rebuild it, renaming it the Orpheum Theatre, the name it still bears. During the time that the reconstruction was underway, a competitor installed and operated the Empress Theater in a small building that was the first Babbitt Brothers Garage. The site of this short-lived theater is now the Empress Theater Parking Lot on Aspen Ave.

Map #19. Coalter Building
1 E. Aspen Avenue
1898

This was Flagstaff's first Post Office building. T. J. Coalter, the owner of the building, was Postmaster, before which he ran a restaurant and the Bank Hotel.

Before 1898 the Post Office was simply a nook in a store. Usually the Postmaster was a store owner, who provided space.

Constructed: 1903
Style: Commercial
Original Use: Bank

This building was originally constructed as the home of the Citizen's Bank by **E. S. Gosney** and F.W. Perkins. For years the bank played a major role in providing capital for area development.

The story of Gosney is the continuing story of sheep ranching in Flagstaff, in which Gosney played a major role. As we saw at Building 12, the first sheep were brought into Flagstaff in 1876. More were soon to follow, especially after the arrival of the railroad made transportation of wool and meat convenient and inexpensive. The open range conditions prevailed through the 1880s and 1890s and prices were protected by tariffs, making sheep production a profitable business.

Others were quick to notice these profits and began coming to the area, causing exponential growth, as shown by the following figures for sheep around Flagstaff: 1876—10,000, 1880—76,524, 1890—698,404. The sheep industry was the largest employer in northern Arizona, providing the only way for many people in the area to make a living. This prosperity lurched to a halt in the Panic of 1893, and many sheepmen went broke.

Those who survived were shocked when Con-

Address:
17 N. Leroux Street

Remodeled: 1940s, 1980s
Style: Spanish Influence
Present Use: Stilley Building

gress passed the Forest Reserves Act in 1896. They correctly feared that this would be used as a vehicle by anti-sheep interests to stop sheep grazing on Federal lands. In order to handle this threat, they organized the Arizona Wool Growers Association in 1898 and elected E. S. Gosney as President. Gosney was a lawyer, banker, sheepman and friend of Gifford Pinchot, who was the "Father of the Forest Service" and a powerful advisor to President McKinley. Gosney convinced Pinchot to conduct a scientific study of the effects of sheep grazing rather than relying on rumors and unsupported claims.

Pinchot undertook the study, the results of which vindicated the sheepmen. This staved off the first threat. However, when Teddy Roosevelt became President in 1901 after McKinley was assassinated, sheep foes secretly approached Roosevelt and secured an order banning sheep grazing.

Gosney immediately called on Pinchot to present the president with his grazing study and Roosevelt had the courage to rescind his order, thereby saving the sheep industry, the economy of northern Arizona and the future of Flagstaff.

HOTEL WEATHERFORD

Constructed: 1898 and 1899
Style: Victorian
Original Use: Shop, Then Hotel

John W. Weatherford, the builder of this hotel, came to Flagstaff in 1886 in a horse and buggy. He traded the buggy to Sandy Donahue for a couple of lots on Gold Avenue (later called Leroux Street) and began his Flagstaff career. At first he ran the Parlor Saloon, then a hack line to Mill Town, then a livery stable. Finally he found his calling as a merchant, successfully running a Gent's Furnishings store for many years.

He built the south half of this building in 1898 as a store, then added the north part in 1899, converting the whole into a hotel that opened for business on January 1, 1900.

Until 1927 when it was eclipsed by the Monte Vista Hotel (Building 29) this was Flagstaff's best hotel. Zane Grey stayed here while he wrote *The Call of the Canyon*. Other famous visitors were William Randolph Hearst and Theodore Roosevelt.

Encouraged by the success of his hotel and reflecting the confidence that characterized Flagstaff in that era, Weatherford became a builder. In 1909 he constructed the office for the first telephone company in Flagstaff, Building 16. From this he went on to build Flagstaff's first cinema in

Address:
21-23 N. Leroux Street

Remodeled: 1929
Style: Same
Present Use: Hotel and Cafe

1911, the Majestic, rebuilt in 1916 after snow collapsed the roof. Now named the Orpheum Theatre, it is Building 18. Finally he embarked upon the building venture that was to be his crowning triumph, the Weatherford Road.

The Weatherford Road was a scenic auto toll road to the top of the San Francisco Peaks. Weatherford secured Forest Service permits for construction but was short of funds. He tried to raise money by selling stock to local residents but the stock sales were meager. Doggedly, he carried on with his own money.

After years of effort, he completed the road in 1926. When the Great Depression hit, Weatherford had over-extended himself, borrowing against his other properties to finance the road. As a result, he was wiped out through mortgage foreclosures in 1932 and died almost penniless in 1934.

The hotel had a beautiful tower and balcony as you see in the old photo. Over the years it fell into disrepair and finally had to be removed. The present owners hope to rebuild it.

Map Number 20:
Pollock Building

Constructed: 1900 -1903
Style: Commercial
Original Use: Shops

If you look carefully as you stand in front of this building you will see how it is joined to the Coalter Building. The brick used on both buildings is the same and the brickwork (some of which is ornate and nicely done) was intended to match, although it isn't a perfect blend.

The first part of this building, the ground floor, was built in 1900 by B. A. Sanderson. T. E. Pollock took over the ownership in 1902 and added the second story, finishing it in 1903.

T. E. Pollock was a banker, who came to Flagstaff in 1895. He took over operation of the Arizona Central Bank and made it into a very successful business.

After learning about local industries through his banking transactions, he tried his hand at ranching, and began buying land, cattle and sheep. In a short time he became one of the largest ranchers in northern Arizona.

Next he turned his attentions to the lumber business. His study convinced him that what was needed was a really large operation that could employ economies of scale. He made some local lumber investments and then went to the White Mountains of eastern Arizona and built a huge mill

**Remodeled: 1903 (2d Story Added)
Style: Commercial
Present Use: Cafe and Shops**

there. The mill town later became known as McNary.

The post-war depression of the early 1920s wiped out his first fortune. He proceeded to build another, only to lose it in the Great Depression of the 1930s.

Pollock continued in banking until the 1920s, wisely getting out of the business before 1929. When the Arizona Central Bank failed, Pollock led the fight to recover money for its depositors. He was credited with having won for them the recovery of fifty-one percent of their deposits, whereas without his help they would have received only twenty per cent.

He was on his way to making his third fortune when he died in 1938.

The Phoenix newspaper's obituary said, *"Mr. Pollock was lauded as having done more for Northern Arizona during his 43 years of residence than any other man through building up the lumbering and livestock industries and financing the ventures of others."*

Constructed: 1907 and 1911
Style: Commercial
Original Use: Offices, Shops & Post Office

As we arrive at these buildings, we meet the Babbitt family, which has figured so large in the history of Flagstaff. The Babbitts came here from Cincinnati, Ohio, five brothers who had a thirst to get into the cattle business in the West. **David Babbitt**, the oldest, scouted various Western locations in 1884. The brothers decided to move to New Mexico, liquidated their Ohio holdings and sent David and William west with $20,000. The two brothers found land prices along the Rio Grande too high and decided not to invest there. Acting on a ticket agent's tip, they investigated Flagstaff.

They arrived in Flagstaff on April 7, 1886, liked the look of the place and decided to stay, joined eventually by the other brothers. Plunging into the acquisition of land and cattle, the Babbitts called their operation the CO Bar, after their home town, Cincinnati, Ohio. It became a famous brand.

The ranch had some lean years in its beginning period, so David and George started independent businesses while Charles and William ran the ranch. George opened the town's first soda fountain on Railroad Avenue (the former Front Street) and was a bookkeeper for P. J. Brannen.

Address:
15-25 E. Aspen Avenue

Remodeled: None
Style: Same
Present Use: Shops

David bought several lots along Aspen Avenue. He built a lumber yard where Building 23 is now, and ran a very successful operation, underpricing his competitors by buying carload lots of merchandise—an innovation. In 1888 he erected a fine red sandstone building on the site. Things went so well that the other brothers joined in the business in 1889, calling it Babbitt Brothers.

Years later David developed the two buildings we are now visiting. The lower building was built in 1907 as the second Post Office. The higher building was built in 1911. Although the two share a common appearance, the Post Office building was made of conventional masonry while the higher building is made of a cast iron frame with masonry curtain walls. Tufa is used in both. The buildings make a hollow square within which is a hidden courtyard accessible through the alley.

David Babbitt was the mastermind of the Babbitt Brothers' commercial operations. He was well loved, for although he became well-to-do, he was always modest in his ways. He was also a patron of the arts and supported many cultural activities. When he died in 1929, he left a legacy of business ability, philanthropy and civic responsibility.

Map Number 23:
Babbitt Brothers Building

Constructed: 1888
Style: Renaissance Revival
Original Use: Store

This grand old building is one of the town's prize pieces of architecture, a wonderful example of the use of the native red Moencopi sandstone. Before the Coconino County Courthouse was built in 1894, the county offices were located on the second floor of this building. The town's first opera house was located upstairs also.

We have already met David Babbitt. He and his brother George guided the operation of the store located here. William and Charles devoted their time to the livestock operations while Edward, an attorney, took care of legal matters. Edward returned to Cincinnati in 1891.

In time, the Babbitts became involved in an amazing number of businesses, everything from a mortuary to a fox farm. On this block they had their retail store, a packing plant, a lard works, warehouses and an ice plant.

Although ranching in Flagstaff started with sheep, cattle ranching became dominant and the Babbitts were the largest of all operators, buying out the A-1, Hashknife and other outfits. In time they had over a million acres in several states and were constantly expanding.

The momentum created by the original broth-

**Remodeled: 1891, 1904, 1957
Style: Restored
Present Use: Stores, Apartments, Offices**

ers crested in 1956, when Charles, the last of them, died. By then their stores were all over northern Arizona and the appearance of the Babbitt name on businesses throughout Flagstaff gave the impression that they owned the town. There was an old Flagstaff saying about this time, that even the sheep said, "Baa-bbitt."

Since then the second and third Babbitt generations have cut back operations considerably. The warehouses and packing plant were removed from this block. The Ford agency was moved. Finally the only Babbitt business left downtown was the old Babbitt Brothers department store. When finally even this landmark store was closed in 1987, it was a dark time for downtown Flagstaff. For one hundred years Babbitts' building had been the mainstay of the downtown area.

Citizens noted with interest in 1989 that Charles's grandson, Jim, had purchased the building, then perked up as he announced a plan to strip away a 1957 "improved" facing, and finally watched spellbound in 1990 as the grand old red stone building underneath was revealed bit by bit. This beautiful restoration lit a fire under the revival of the historic downtown district.

Map Number 24:
Babbitts' Garage

Constructed: 1915
Style: Commercial
Original Use: Garage & Auto Dealership

This building continues the Babbitt saga.

In 1915 the Babbitts were involved in the horse and buggy business in many ways: they sold buggies, tack and feed and had a livery stable. There were only a couple of dozen cars in town and there were no paved streets. Some of the town leaders were promoting Flagstaff as a stop along the proposed National Old Trails Highway but this highway-to-be was then nothing but a loose collection of unpaved roads. It was a rare and hardy traveler who tried to come to Flagstaff by car.

In spite of those conditions, Edwin Babbitt convinced his reluctant father David to lead the brothers into the automobile business. He first prevailed upon David to buy him a car. The car soon needed repairs; so Edwin wheedled his father into opening a small garage (later the home of the Empress Theater). Having had a taste of the auto business, the Babbitts plunged into it by building this substantial structure, gambling on the future.

The National Old Trails Highway was built. Motorists began to come through the area, first in a trickle and then in a flood. Flagstaff's tourism industry skyrocketed. The National Old Trails Highway became Route 66, the glory days of

Remodeled: 1992-1993
Style: Same
Present Use: Offices

which were in the 1930s through 1960s. Now Route 66 has been replaced by Interstate-40. Through it all, Flagstaff, due to its strategic cross-roads location, has benefited enormously from the millions of automobile travelers who drive through the area.

The Babbitt Brothers landed a Ford franchise for their new automobile business, which soon became a hot ticket at a time when the word "Ford" was a synonym for "car."

Edwin's foresight paid off handsomely.

This building marks a first in Flagstaff, the use of a reinforced concrete frame. The loads are borne by enormous reinforced concrete pillars and beams, the brick walls being mere curtains. The building was renovated by the Aspey, Watkins & Diesel law firm in 1992-1993. As the contractor dug into the old building, he was astonished at its solid structure. The Babbitts had little guidance on how to construct such a building so they overbuilt it.

After Babbitt Ford moved into a new location in 1959, this large old building was used as a retail store, then a storage facility, and then sank into dereliction. Now it is a shining example of conscientious recycling.

Constructed: 1894
Style: Romanesque Revival
Original Use: County Offices

Arizona and New Mexico were one territory, and that territory was part of Mexico until 1848 when the United States walked away with most of the land as a prize of the Mexican War. Arizona became a separate territory in 1864 and was so sparsely populated that only four huge counties were carved out of it. Flagstaff was located in Yavapai County, the largest of the four. Chunks of Yavapai were broken off to help form Maricopa, Apache and Gila Counties, but when Flagstaff became a populous settlement in the 1890s, Yavapai County was still enormous. Prescott was the county seat, and getting there from Flagstaff to serve on a jury or take care of business was a long hard journey.

After much pressure was applied by Flagstaff residents, (spearheaded by many of the men we meet on this tour) Coconino County was split from Yavapai County in 1891. The 526 voters participating in a special election that year picked Flagstaff over Williams as the county seat.

In 1891, Arizona was still a federal Territory. The only means by which Coconino County could raise the money to build a courthouse was by issuing bonds, and this required an Act of Con-

Remodeled: Several Times
Style: Mixed
Present Use: County Offices

gress. It seemed that Congress was in no hurry, and it was not until 1894 that it finally approved the measure. Even then the county could not afford to put a clock in the clock tower.

After its creation, Coconino County's population grew constantly, requiring expansion of the courthouse from time to time. The first addition was built in 1925, and followed the original design. Later additions departed from the original look. The 1956 wing, added to the front and to the west face of the building, was modern, ruined the integrity, and went with the old building like "ketchup on ice cream" as *Arizona Daily Sun* newspaper editor Platt Cline put it. Other additions were made in 1968 and 1979.

Today an effort is underway to restore the wonderful old entryway with its fine carvings. The entry is covered by the inharmonious 1956 add-on but you may find it worthwhile to go inside the building and take a look. You will see some nice stone carving. The building is open from 8:00 a.m. to 5:00 p.m. Monday-Friday.

Constructed: 1917
Style: Neoclassical Revival
Original Use: Temple and Offices

Today when we have so many forms of entertainment available to us at the push of a button, it is hard for us to appreciate how our ancestors lived. Before the movies came to town, the citizens of Flagstaff had to provide their own entertainment, and this they did, with great energy.

Newspapers of the old days are full of stories about social activities. There were many teas, dances and balls. Sightseeing excursions to scenic places around town, such as Walnut Canyon and Sunset Crater were arranged. Lovers of literature met and read Shakespeare to each other. Friends had dinners and parties where they played charades and acted out playlets.

Athletic events were popular, especially races run by teams of men pulling fire hose carts. The Fourth of July was always a big event, with citizens taking advantage of Flagstaff's cool weather to stage ball games and other contests in celebration.

Then there were clubs and societies to join. Flagstaff was a great joiner's town, due to a combination of its isolation and the character of its citizens. Virtually every national organization from the Knights of Pythias to the Woodmen of the World found a ready following here. One of the

Remodeled: 1978
Style: Awning Added
Present Use: Temple and Offices

most active orders was the Masonic Lodge.

Before the Masonic Temple was built, the Masons used the upper story of the Town Hall. They took it as an incomplete shell and finished it in return for being allowed to have their meetings there. (You passed the empty lot where the Town Hall stood at 16 North Leroux Street).

Although the Masons had quite a few members, it was not a wealthy lodge. When the time came to leave the Town Hall and build their own temple, they used an innovative idea: they constructed a building that was large enough so that they could rent space to others, and use the rents to pay the construction mortgage.

In the case of the Masons, they picked a prime downtown location and erected a two-story building with a basement. They used the top story for their rituals and rented out the ground floor and basement. They are still following this practice today.

For many years the basement of this building was the home of the Pastime Recreation Parlor, a bowling alley and pool hall.

Map Number 27:
Federal Building

Constructed: 1936
Style: Federal Moderne
Original Use: Post Office

This is the youngest of the historical buildings on the tour. You can see the cornerstone on the south front of the building, showing that construction began in 1936.

As we saw on earlier tour stops, the Federal government was in the habit of leasing its post offices in Flagstaff for ten year terms. When construction on this building began, the Post Office was in Building 36 and its ten year lease would expire in 1937, just as this new Post Office was ready.

The Federal Building marks a departure from Uncle Sam's previous practice of leasing post office sites. In 1936 the Federal government bought this land and built this structure.

On the lintel above the front door you will see the words "Federal Building." In addition to the Post Office, several other Federal offices were located here, such as those of the Forest Service. The Post Office occupied the ground floor and basement while the other offices were located upstairs.

The building is a nice example of the Federal Moderne style, with clean and harmonious lines. Copper sheathing was used on the front, emphasiz-

Address:
114 N. San Francisco Street

Remodeled: None
Style: Same
Present Use: Private Offices

ing the importance of the metal to Arizona's economy. The decision to use copper was boosted by Arizona's mining industry, which was promoting the use of copper wherever and whenever possible during the Great Depression. During those years Arizona's auto license plates were made of copper for this reason.

This building served as Flagstaff's Post Office for twenty-five years, until 1962, when it moved for the sixth time, to the northeast corner of Aspen Avenue and Agassiz Street, and the government went back to the lease method.

In 1988 the town outgrew its post office yet another time and the seventh one was built in East Flagstaff, for the first time in history moving the post office away from the historic downtown area. The 1988 Post Office is now the main office and the 1962 Post Office is still open as a satellite.

In 1984 the government sold the Federal Building to private developers who have converted it into an office building.

The historical photograph shows the Dedication on the steps of the building on May 28, 1937. Several high ranking Federal officials were present, including Jim Farley, U.S. Postmaster General.

Map Number 28:
Riordan-Babbitt Building

Constructed: 1917
Style: Neoclassical Revival
Original Use: Post Office

This was Flagstaff's third Post Office, constructed by T. A. Riordan and David Babbitt. We have already met David Babbitt. Now it is time to meet **T. A. Riordan**, whose story tells us something about Flagstaff's lumber industry.

The first settlers looked on Flagstaff's vast Ponderosa pine forests as a local resource good for fuel and logs for cabin building but not as a commercial material, because there was no way to get lumber to market.

E. A. Ayer, a Chicago businessman, secured a contract with the railroad to build a lumber mill at Flagstaff to supply the line with ties and timbers. Ayer hoped to ship a steam operated saw mill by rail all the way to Flagstaff, only to find the line stalled because the prefabricated bridge that was supposed to span Canyon Diablo was short. Undaunted, Ayer took the mill apart, wrestled the components over the canyon by sheer manpower and brought it on to Flagstaff by ox team. It was Flagstaff's first large commercial lumber mill, beginning operation here in 1882.

Ayer hired D. M. Riordan to manage the mill for him. Five years after operations began, D. M. Riordan bought out Ayer and brought his brothers,

T. A. Riordan and M. J. Riordan into the operation, T. A. and M. J. soon bought out D. M.

Shortly afterwards a fire burned the mill to the ground. The Riordans rebuilt it bigger and better. From 1887 to 1930 (when it closed —a victim of the Great Depression) their Arizona Lumber & Timber Company was Flagstaff's largest lumber mill, furnishing jobs to hundreds of workers. The Riordans acquired timber rights from the Santa Fe on its huge land holdings and ran spur lines into the forests to cut the trees, hauling logs back by rail to the mill to be sawed and finished.

To provide housing for the mill workers, a company town was created known as Mill Town, later Milton (located near today's Milton Road and Riordan Road junction). It had its own commissary and was considered a separate village until 1920 when it was taken into Flagstaff.

T. A. Riordan was a large hearty family man who was an efficient boss but had a compassionate heart. He was very civic minded and participated in virtually every improvement in the town's history during his life. By the time of his death in 1946 he was one of Flagstaff's wealthiest, most influential and best-loved men.

Constructed: 1926
Style: Spanish Influence
Original Use: Hotel

The Monte Vista Hotel is a tribute to Flagstaff's community spirit and a comment on its development from a raw frontier town into a mature community.

Flagstaff enjoyed a boom when cattle and sheep prices soared during World War I, then suffered a bust, as did all America, when a short but sharp depression struck in the early 1920s. Many ranchers and store owners were wiped out, credit was very tight and people hung on to the little they had left, hoping for better times.

Better times came. By 1926 business was picking up and the town's mood was changing from pessimism to optimism. A group of local boosters decided that the time had come to build a first class local hotel. By then the other hotels in Flagstaff were showing their age.

A stock subscription drive was mounted, heralded by a large headline in the local paper, the *Coconino Sun,* on April 2, 1926—**"Do We Want a Hotel?"** The answer was a resounding yes. The promoters were able to raise $200,000 in sixty days—a strong performance considering the size of the town and the small amount of wealth it contained.

Remodeled: None
Style: Same
Present Use: Hotel

Ground was broken in summer 1926 and on January 6, 1927 the hotel was opened for business. Almost every prominent family in town owned stock in the venture. It was a community achievement, and was called The Community Hotel until a name-the-new-hotel contest was held, and a local schoolgirl won the prize for her suggestion Monte Vista, which means *mountain view* in Spanish. The Monte Vista quickly became the center of downtown life. It was the place to go for a dinner, dance or club meeting.

The hotel did well in its first years, paying a yearly ten percent return to investors. By the 1950s it was declining and by the 1960s it had become a white elephant. Disagreement among the stockholders led to one group buying out another.

Finally the stock was consolidated and came into the hands of the present owners, who have restored the building. The new owners pumped money into the operation and refurbished the hotel. Today the Monte Vista is in good condition, once again operating as a centerpiece of downtown Flagstaff.

Map Number 30:
Elks Hall

Constructed: 1899
Style: Commercial
Original Use: Lodge & Shops

This building was constructed by John G. Verkamp and T. A. Rickel, who rented the upper floor to the Elks.

The Elks reached their meeting rooms by means of an outside staircase. After the Elks moved to larger quarters in 1927, the stairs were removed, the upstairs was remodeled into apartments and new brick work was added.

The ground floor tenant was a combination pool hall and confectionery shop.

Pool halls were an old story in Flagstaff, and while they were regarded as dens of iniquity, they were tolerated. Mothers were alarmed, however, to see something new—a bowling alley—go into the basement, worrying that young people, always looking for newfangled and exciting things, would be debauched by it. They were concerned not only for their own children but also for the students who would soon be coming to town to attend the new Northern Arizona Normal School (later to become NAU). In spite of their opposition, bowling stayed, followed soon by—shudder—the movies.

In the Teens, the ground floor of the Elks Building was taken over by a drug store, which changed hands over the years. In the 1930s it

became Moore Drug. You can still see a sign that was painted in 1938 by Flagstaff sign painter Jack Fuss for Moore Drug on the wall facing Aspen Avenue.

By the time this building was constructed, the character of downtown had developed into a pattern that lasted for decades: the area along Route 66 was for travelers and those who frequented the saloons; while the area where you are standing, Aspen Avenue running from San Francisco Street to Leroux Street, was the part of town used by the locals. If a resident talked of going downtown, this would be the area the person had in mind.

Downtown suffered for a while after chain stores and shopping malls came into Flagstaff in the 1970s, and there was a shakeout during which some of the old-line family businesses moved or closed down.

Today downtown is reviving and entrepreneurs are learning how to find successful niches that can compete with the giant stores. Downtown provides the perfect setting for these small and unique operations, making it an interesting and worthwhile place to visit, with the added bonus of history that is lacking in the malls.

Map #31. Coconino Sun Building
111 E. Aspen Avenue
1926

Flagstaff's first real newspaper was *The Champion*, a weekly. Afterwards it became *The Coconino Sun*. Later the paper changed its format and title to the *Arizona Daily Sun*, the name it still bears.

The *Sun* building was located on the north side of Aspen Avenue. The editor of the *Sun* was one of the principal boosters of the construction of the Monte Vista hotel, Building 29, only to learn that the hotel would need the space that the *Sun* occupied. With a fine spirit of cooperation, the *Sun* erected this new building and moved into it, allowing the Monte Vista to be built.

Map #32. Bikker Building #1
113 E. Aspen Avenue
1917

This building has an unusual exterior: river pebbles have been embedded in concrete to give it a jewelled appearance. Underneath the pebbles lies an 1880s building that was used as a harness shop.

Map #33. Bikker Building #2
117 E. Aspen Avenue
1917

The first floor of this building was built to house the J. C. Penney store, which was the first of the national chain stores to come to Flagstaff. Penney's used the glazed yellow and orange tiles that you will see on the front of the building as a trademark. In a couple of years Penney's moved to the Masonic Temple, Building Number 26. In 1920 the upper story was added and used as the Odd Fellows' Hall.

Map #34. Hawks Building
14 N. San Francisco St.
1897

J. F. "Dad" Hawks was one of Flagstaff's first settlers, coming here in 1881. He set up a restaurant in a tent in Old Town. He followed the move to New Town and spent a long career in the restaurant business.

Hawks was the father of the two boys shot by the lynch mob. See Building 10.

Map #35. Finley Building
1913

See the article on page 58.

Map #36. Nackard Building
13-15 N. San Francisco St.
1922

K. J. Nackard came to Flagstaff in 1912 and quickly made his mark. He occupied the old Brannen properties (Buildings 3-5) and remodelled them, setting up a business called the New York Store.

He was so successful that he built this new place and moved the store here. The facing is made of an unusual glazed white brick. This was Post Office #4.

Map #37. New Babbitt Building
6-10 N. San Francisco St.
1935

The Babbitts took over the old Brannen properties from K.J. Nackard, then built this structure on the northern part of the Brannen lots, tying the whole property together with a yellow brick facing.

The Babbitts located Flagstaff's first TV studio upstairs in this building, a low-wattage cable operation, in the early 1950s.

Map Number 35:
Finley Building

Constructed: 1913
Style: Commercial
Original Use: Store

Sam Finley was a character. He came to Flagstaff about the turn of the century and operated a small secondhand store located in a shack on this lot.

Early pictures of the store make one wonder how he could have made a living out of such a humble place, but Finley bought, sold, swapped and finagled. He had a dream of buying the land on which the shack was located and building the tallest building in the county on it.

Through a combination of thrift, shrewd merchandising and charm, he was able to make enough money to carry out his dream. Locating a team of brick masons, he set out to construct his dream building, and up it went in 1913.

You will see in the old photograph that Finley loved to display his name. It was painted in large letters all over his store. He also loved to write bad poetry, and ran a series of ads using jingles that he composed. He even put out his own little newsletter full of the poems. High on the north wall of the building he painted one of his poems, which you can see in the historic photo on page 38. When William Switzer bought the building in 1920, he painted over part of Finley's poem, but you can

Remodeled: Slight changes
Style: Same
Present Use: Gallery

still see some of the original letters.

This is the poem on the wall:

A Flagite was poor,

But his troubles are o'er.

He has money to burn,

Since he trades at this store.

Finley's new store did well. He served as Flagstaff's mayor twice, in 1916 and 1918, then moved to California in 1921.

William Switzer, a Flagstaff pioneer, moved his hardware store into the Finley Building and ran it there for 58 years, closing it in 1978. Since then the building has been used as a restaurant, a shop and a gallery.

———

You have now almost completed the loop back to the starting point, and have seen how Flagstaff grew and developed as a town.

We hope you have enjoyed your stroll, and for visitors and residents alike, we hope you now have a better understanding and appreciation of Flagstaff's Downtown Historic District.

Hidden Flagstaff

Beneath your feet as you have walked through downtown is hidden Flagstaff.

During Flagstaff's formative years, it was the practice to build a full basement in each of the buildings. In those parts of the downtown where the buildings are lined up shoulder to shoulder, especially along Route 66 between San Francisco and Leroux Streets, and the buildings are single-story, there is as much structural space below ground as there is above. The basements are separated by walls, often sharing a party wall. Therefore it is an easy matter to link basements together by breaking holes in the walls.

The first residents to take advantage of this feature were Flagstaff's Chinese community. They were engaged in the pursuits that were usual to the Chinese in Western towns, running cafes and laundries. The Chinese were blamed for the first big fire in New Town, in 1886, and many of them were driven away. Some returned after feelings had cooled down, but they were understandably cautious about further reprisals. For protection, they dug secret tunnels connecting the basements of their businesses. These ran primarily between the places shown as Buildings 6-11 on the map.

Years later another series of tunnels came into being as a by-product of Flagstaff's first electric plant, which was The Flagstaff Electric Light Company, created in 1895. (Among the incorporators were David Babbitt, T. A. Riordan and Sandy Donahue.)

The company built a small power plant where the Blome Building now stands on the NAU campus. In 1913 it built a larger plant at 116 W. Phoenix Avenue.

The plant was steam driven, pushing the steam through turbines to generate electricity.

In order to take advantage of the steam, the Flagstaff Steam Laundry was installed in the upper floor of the power plant, but even so, excess steam was released unused into the air.

Then the plant manager came up with an

ingenious and ecologically sound idea to provide heat to the community as well as power. Steam was captured after it passed through the turbines and carried through a series of pipes to the downtown buildings, where it was used to provide heat through radiators. The cooled steam was returned to the plant as distilled water, to be boiled again, generating more steam. Fuel for the boilers was sawmill waste: wood chunks, slabs, etc. It worked beautifully, and in time virtually every business in downtown Flagstaff was on line.

The steam pipeline went underground from the plant to downtown and a series of tunnels was built in 1920 to house the steam lines and to give access to them for repairs and maintenance. Each business on line had a door into the tunnel through its basement. This created the second network of tunnels. It was during the construction of this network that the secret Chinese tunnels were discovered.

Yet a third tunnel system was created by the Babbitts. In 1921 the Babbitts formed their own company to provide power and steam heat. They dug extensive tunnels for the steam pipes under their own properties, in places connecting their tunnels with the downtown tunnel system.

As a result of these various tunnel networks connecting the downtown buildings through their basements, a virtual underground city was created.

From time to time through the years, people have gone into these tunnels for various reasons and have discovered secret hideaways containing everything from opium pipes, to moonshine to a cache of slot machines.

The tunnels are not open to the public.

(In 1945, Arizona Public Service Company bought out the local power company. In 1949, natural gas came to town. These two developments spelled the end for the steam system, which shut down in 1966. The power plant was demolished in the late 1960s.)

Further Exploration

1. Flagstaff Historical Monument–Walk

Start at Flagstaff City Hall, at the corner of Humphreys Street and Aspen Avenue. Walk west on Aspen. At the end of the block you will see the historic Milligan House made of Flagstaff red brick. Milligan ran the brick works. Cross over Sitgreaves Street and turn right, walking north on the west side of Sitgreaves St. Across Aspen Avenue you will see the historic Federated Church, a lovely Moencopi sandstone structure.

Continue walking north on Sitgreaves St. until you come to Dale Avenue. Turn left (west) at the footbridge and then right (north) on the dirt path between the fences. The path takes you along the east bank of the Rio de Flag.

At Bonito St. you will see signs for the Urban Trail System and the trail is gravel surfaced. Follow the trail as it winds around City Pond and then turns north. Just beyond the pond you will see the monument, which looks like a phone pole on a stone base. The walk is 0.75 miles each way.

2. Nob Hill–Walk

Starting in the downtown area, at Aspen Avenue and Leroux Street, walk north on Leroux St. to the top of the hill, four blocks. You will see some large old homes, as Leroux Street was considered a choice location, where the "nobs" lived. The T. E. Pollock Mansion is at 410 N. Leroux. The home of John Weatherford is at 421 N. Leroux, and in front of it you will see the last hitching post in Flagstaff, a concrete post with an iron ring on top.

3. Riordan Mansion–Drive

The twin homes of brother lumber barons T. A. and M. J. Riordan have been preserved as a State Park and guided tours are given throughout the day. The address is 1300 Riordan Ranch Road. Phone 779-4395.

4. Pioneer Historical Museum–Drive

This is located in the 1908 County Hospital Building. Exhibits and information. Located at 2340 North Ft. Valley Road. Phone 774-6272.

5. Old Town Spring–Drive

From City Hall, go west on Route 66 for a half block. Do not turn left (south) under the overpass. Instead, keep going straight ahead on Santa Fe.

Turn left (south) at Park Street, at 0.2 miles. Turn right immediately and go west to West Lower Coconino Avenue at 0.4 miles from City Hall. Turn left here, then right, and follow West Lower Coconino Avenue to the 0.55 mile point, where you will see La Plaza Vieja, a small park, to your right. Drive up to the swing set and park.

You will find a plaque by the flag staff. It has a nice historic photo of Old Town. The spring is defined by a circle of stones, with a channel leading downhill to the railroad.

5. Lowell Observatory–Drive

Percival Lowell, a wealthy New Englander, was an astronomer who believed that there was life on Mars. To prove his theories, he scoured the globe to find an observatory site that was just right for "good seeing." Flagstaff was on his list.

Lowell chose Flagstaff and set up the observatory in 1894. During his life the facility concentrated on Mars studies, but since his death in 1916, it has broadened its interests. The planet Pluto was discovered here in 1930.

Tours are given and on some nights visitors can look through a telescope.

Lowell Observatory is located atop Mars Hill. Call 774-2096 for information

6. Museum of Northern Arizona–Drive

Harold Colton, like Lowell, was a wealthy Easterner interested in science. In 1926 he moved to Flagstaff to devote his life to studying the region.

Colton found so much interesting material that he decided to create a museum. His first museum was housed near downtown, in 1928. It was moved to its present quarters north of town in 1936 and has become one of the finest regional museums in the country.

It is located three miles north on Highway 180. Phone 774-5211 for information.

Bibliography

Ashworth, Donna.
> *Biography of a Small Mountain.*
> Flagstaff: Small Mountain Books,
> 1992.

Cline, Platt.
> *They Came to the Mountain.* Flagstaff:
> Northland Press, 1976.
> *Mountain Town.* Flagstaff: Northland
> Press, 1993.

Flagstaff: 1876-1976. Flagstaff Symphony
> Guild. Flagstaff: Northland Press,
> 1976.

Hochderffer, George.
> *Flagstaff Whoa.* Flagstaff: Northland
> Press, 1965.

Janus Design.
> *Railroad Addition Historic District.*
> Tempe: Flagstaff Historic Sites
> Commission, 1979.

McNary, James.
> *This is My Life.* Albuquerque: U. of
> New Mexico Press, 1956.

Flagstaff, Arizona 1897. Flagstaff: Northland
> Press, 1975.

Smith, Dean.
> *Brothers Five.* Tempe:Arizona Histori-
> cal Foundation, 1989.

Sykes, Godfrey.
> *A Westerly Trend.* Tucson: Arizona
> Pioneers Historical Society, 1944.

Tinker, George.
> *Northern Arizona in 1887.* Glendale,
> California: Arthur H. Clark Company,
> 1969.

Trimble, Marshall.
> *CO Bar.* Flagstaff: Northland Press,
> 1982.

Archives of Flagstaff newspapers on microfilm:
> Flagstaff Public Library
> NAU Cline Library

Journal of Arizona History, various issues
